DOGS SET V

Great Danes

Julie Murray
ABDO Publishing Company

visit us at
www.abdopub.com

Published by ABDO Publishing Company, 4940 Viking Drive, Edina, Minnesota 55435.
Copyright © 2003 by Abdo Consulting Group, Inc. International copyrights reserved in
all countries. No part of this book may be reproduced in any form without written
permission from the publisher.

Printed in the United States.

Cover Photo: Ron Kimball
Interior Photos: Animals Animals pp. 7, 9, 15, 21; Corbis pp. 5, 13, 19;
    Ron Kimball pp. 11, 17

Contributing Editors: Kate A. Conley, Kristin Van Cleaf, Kristianne E. Vieregger
Art Direction & Graphics: Neil Klinepier

Library of Congress Cataloging-in-Publication Data

Murray, Julie, 1969-
    Great Danes / Julie Murray.
        p. cm. -- (Dogs Set V)
    Summary: An introduction to the physical characteristics, behavior, and proper care
  of Great Danes.
    Includes bibliographical references (p.).
    ISBN 1-57765-923-6
    1. Great Dane--Juvenile literature. [1. Great Dane. 2. Dogs.] I. Title.

SF429.G7 M87 2003
636.73--dc21   2002074655

Contents

The Dog Family

Dogs and humans have been living together for thousands of years. Dogs were first tamed about 12,000 years ago. They were used as guards, hunters, and companions.

Today, about 400 different dog **breeds** exist. They can differ greatly in appearance. Some can weigh as much as 200 pounds (91 kg). Others are small enough to fit in the palms of your hands.

Despite these differences, all dogs belong to the same scientific **family**. It is called Canidae. This name comes from the Latin word *canis*, which means dog.

The Canidae family includes more than just **domestic** dogs. Foxes, jackals, coyotes, and wolves belong to this family, too. In fact, many people believe today's domestic dogs descended from wolves.

Wolves have many characteristics in common with Great Danes.

Great Danes

People have **bred** Great Danes for nearly 400 years. Many people believe that this breed began in Denmark. That's because people from Denmark are called Danes. But in fact, this breed actually began in Germany.

In Germany, this breed was known as the *Deutsche Dogge*, which means "German mastiff." But one French name for this breed was *Grand Danois*, which means "big Danish." The English **translated** this into Great Dane. Today, English speakers still use this name.

Great Danes are descendants of English mastiffs and Irish wolfhounds. They were originally bred to hunt wild boars and other animals. Today, Great Danes are mainly companion dogs.

Sometimes Great Danes are called Gentle Giants.

What They're Like

Great Danes are known as the **Apollo** of Dogs. Like Apollo, these large dogs are considered to have a strong, noble character. They can be clumsy as puppies, but grow to become elegant adults. They are sweet and loving dogs.

Great Danes can be wary of strangers. While their large size and bark may scare an **intruder**, Great Danes are not usually aggressive. However, they do need strict training as puppies. With proper training and treatment, Great Danes are gentle and well behaved.

This **breed** usually gets along well with children and other pets. Great Danes can be very sensitive. They enjoy being inside a home and part of a family. They can also be very protective and loyal.

A merle-colored Great Dane has a gray body with black spots. A Great Dane with this color coat cannot compete in dog shows, but it can still be a loyal and loving pet.

Coat and Color

The Great Dane's coat is short and **dense**. Its hair is smooth and glossy. The **American Kennel Club** recognizes five Great Dane colors. They are brindle, fawn, black, harlequin, and blue.

Brindle-colored coats are a golden color with black stripes. Fawn is a golden-tan color. Dogs with brindle or fawn coats have black masks on their faces.

A black Great Dane has a glossy, pure-black coat. A harlequin-colored dog has a white coat with black patches on most of its body. A blue Great Dane has a steel blue coat.

The Great Dane's eyes are usually dark. It often has a black nose. However, a harlequin dog may sometimes have a spotted nose. A blue Great Dane may have a steel blue-colored nose.

These fawn-colored Great Danes each have a mask of darker color.

Size

The Great Dane is one of the largest dog **breeds**. It is a giant! The average Great Dane stands between 28 and 32 inches (71 and 81 cm) tall at the shoulder. It can weigh between 100 and 150 pounds (45 and 68 kg). A female Great Dane is usually smaller than a male.

The Great Dane has a huge body with a long, rectangular head. This breed is strong and powerful, but it also has great elegance. The Great Dane's tail is long, with a slight curve at the end.

A Great Dane has high-set, medium-size ears. They naturally hang down close to the cheeks. But some people prefer to crop the ears.

Cropping is cutting a Great Dane's ears so they come to a point. The dog's ears are then taped to

stand up straight. After a while, the ears stand up without help. A **veterinarian** usually crops a puppy's ears after it is seven weeks old.

Other dog breeds look tiny compared to the Great Dane.

Care

The Great Dane is easy to groom. Once a week, brush its coat with a rubber brush. It is also good to clean your dog's teeth and clip its nails regularly.

A Great Dane's ears need regular cleaning. To do this, moisten a cotton ball with a special solution for cleaning a dog's ears. Then, gently wipe the inside of the ear. Clean ears are less likely to become infected.

Watch your Great Dane for signs of **bloat**. A dog with bloat has a swollen stomach, and is usually restless and uncomfortable. This condition can be fatal if it is not treated quickly by a **veterinarian**.

Your Great Dane also needs to visit the veterinarian at least once a year for a checkup. He or she can check your dog for illnesses and give it shots to prevent diseases. If you are not going to **breed** your dog, have the veterinarian **spay** or **neuter** it.

Since Great Danes are so large, they can accidentally do a lot of damage. They need plenty of space and proper training to make good pets.

Feeding

An adult Great Dane's daily food allowance should be divided into two meals. This will prevent your dog from eating too quickly. Eating or drinking too quickly, or exercising after eating, may cause **bloat**.

Dog food can be dry, moist, or semimoist. Most dogs will eat a high-quality, dry dog food. Others prefer to have some canned food mixed in with their dry food. To help prevent bloat, dry food can be mixed with a little water to soften it.

Choose a brand and type of food your Great Dane enjoys and stick with it. Changes in diet should be made gradually to prevent stomach problems.

A dog also needs fresh, clean water every day. Your dog will also like treats. But only give your dog treats occasionally. This will keep your dog healthy.

A Great Dane's food should be raised off the floor on a special rack. That way, this tall dog will not have to bend down too far when eating.

Things They Need

The Great Dane is happiest as an inside dog. You can create your dog's own space in the house by supplying the dog with a large crate. Your Great Dane will also need a soft, comfortable blanket or cushion to lie on. Otherwise, it may get **calluses**.

A Great Dane needs regular exercise. It needs a large yard with a tall fence in which to run and play. It also likes long, daily walks.

Every dog should wear a collar with two tags. One tag shows the dog has had its shots. The other tag shows the dog's name and its owner's address and phone number. A dog can also have a **tattoo** or **microchip** for identification.

Great Dane puppies need proper nutrition and exercise to grow into healthy adults.

Puppies

Baby dogs are called puppies. A mother dog is usually **pregnant** for about nine weeks. A Great Dane can have about six to eight puppies in a **litter**.

Puppies are born blind and deaf. Their eyes and ears will begin working when they are about two weeks old. They can walk at three weeks, and they are usually **weaned** at about seven weeks of age.

Puppies can be given away or sold when they are about eight weeks old. If you are going to buy a **purebred** puppy, make sure to buy it from a qualified **breeder**. Many puppies and older dogs are also available from the **Humane Society**.

Opposite page: Great Dane puppies need to drink their mother's milk for the first seven weeks of their lives.

It is important to take your puppy to the **veterinarian**. He or she will give your puppy the shots it needs to stay healthy. A puppy should start getting these shots when it is between six and eight weeks old. A healthy Great Dane will live about seven years.

Glossary

American Kennel Club - a club that studies, breeds, and exhibits purebred dogs.

Apollo - the god of the sun in Greek mythology.

bloat - a condition in which air gets trapped in a dog's stomach, causing pain, shock, and even death.

breed - a group of dogs sharing the same appearance and characteristics. A breeder is a person who raises dogs. Raising dogs is often called breeding them.

callus - a hard, thick area of skin.

dense - thick.

domestic - living with humans.

family - a group that scientists use to classify similar plants and animals. It ranks above a genus and below an order.

Humane Society - an organization that cares for and protects animals.

intruder - a person who enters an area, such as another person's home, without permission.

litter - all the puppies born at one time to a mother dog.

microchip - a small computer chip. A veterinarian inserts the chip between a dog's shoulder blades. If the dog is lost, the Humane Society can scan the chip to find the dog's identification information and owners.

neuter - to remove a male animal's reproductive parts.

pregnant - having one or more babies growing within the body.

purebred - an animal whose parents are both from the same breed.

spay - to remove a female animal's reproductive parts.

tattoo - a permanent design made on the skin. An owner can have an identification number tattooed on the leg of his or her dog.

translate - to change from one language to another.

veterinarian - a doctor who cares for animals.

wean - to accustom an animal to eating food other than its mother's milk.

Web Sites

Would you like to learn more about Great Danes? Please visit **www.abdopub.com** to find up-to-date Web site links about dog care and the Great Dane breed. These links are routinely monitored and updated to provide the most current information available.

Index

J
636.73
M

Murray, Julie,
1969-
    Great Danes

p2/35   11/03

The Bryant Library
Roslyn, New York
(516) 621-2240